BEHOLD!

CULTIVATING ATTENTIVENESS
IN THE SEASON OF ADVENT

PAMELA C. HAWKINS

UPPER
ROOM BOOKS®
NASHVILLE

BEHOLD!

Cultivating Attentiveness in the Season of Advent
© 2011 by Pamela C. Hawkins. All rights reserved.

The Upper Room Web site: http://www.upperroom.org
Cover design: Bruce Gore | GoreStudio.com

LIBRARY OF CONGRESS CATALOGING-IN-PUBLICATION DATA
Hawkins, Pamela C.
    Behold!: cultivating attentiveness in the season of Advent / Pamela C. Hawkins.
       p. cm
    ISBN: 978-0-8358-1062-3
    1. Advent—Prayers and devotions. 2. Bible—Devotional literature. 3. Common lectionary (1992). Year B. I. Title
    BV40.H38 2011
    242'.332—dc22

                                                            2011002962

Printed in the United States of America

To my husband,

RAY,

whose promises are breath and earth for me.

CONTENTS

INTRODUCTION

*Be not afraid; for behold, I bring you good news of a great joy
which will come to all the people; for to you is born this day in
the city of David a Savior, who is Christ the Lord.*

—LUKE 2:10, RSV

Behold is a word that softens the edges of my heart. I cannot
say this word without moving, without extending and lifting a
hand, palm open, toward the object of my attention. *Behold* is a
word of weight, a word that carries itself differently for me than
does the word *see.* If it is said with intent, urgency, or wonder,
see can get my attention; but when I hear the word *behold,* my
attention comes from a different place, a deeper place, as though
I am being invited to see by means of an inner vision.

During the Advent seasons of my childhood, I became
acquainted with this word. It seemed to punctuate the Bible
stories read in Sunday school and worship as Christmas drew
closer; and even then, even when other words did not catch my
youthful attention, something about hearing the preacher or
parent or teacher say, "Behold," changed them when they said

it and changed me when I heard it. It is a word to lean into, a word with reach; it is at once an urgent word but not frightening at all. The word still pulls me toward it in an attitude of curious expectancy and trustful anticipation. I look forward to hearing it spoken and to seeing what it points to. Most of the time, it points me toward God in one breathtaking way or another.

Many modern Bible translations no longer use the word *behold*. As one who loves and works with words, I have a deep appreciation for biblical and linguistic scholarship that continues to teach us about the language of our faith. Still, I confess that I miss hearing "behold" read during Advent, and as I prepared to write this resource, it is the word that continued to surface in my memory as I read through the scriptures of the season. *Behold* surfaced not because of its presence in the readings but its presence in my inner life. All the scripture readings for this Advent seemed to call me to an attitude and posture of new attentiveness: Second Samuel, the Psalms, Isaiah, Mark, and Luke. As I reviewed my notes, I noticed a pattern. My writing focused on seeing new things in old texts, asking new questions about old assumptions. The texts drew me to a new Advent attentiveness to the Word and to God's promise of Immanuel. And there it was, in my personal reflections: "Behold"—God was doing a new thing in me as I read these texts that I had read so many times before.

So through this resource, I invite you to "behold" the Word with new eyes, new ears, new hearts, and new possibilities. I hope that you will become freshly open to "behold" the ancient Advent story of God's self-giving of Immanuel, the Word made flesh, and to cultivate an ongoing attentiveness to what God has promised, is promising, and will promise to do in the world in the name, power, and spirit of Jesus the Christ.

And above all, I hope that in some way, this book will encourage and help you "behold" the "good news of a great joy," Christ the Lord, who is coming to make all things new!

How *Behold!* Came to Be

A few years ago I wrote a book titled *Simply Wait: Cultivating Stillness in the Season of Advent.* I had hoped that it would be a useful Advent resource for any year, even though the scripture readings and weekly themes were drawn from Year C of the Revised Common Lectionary. Many people found *Simply Wait* to be useful in this way, but the acquisitions editor asked me to consider writing a companion book for Year B of the Revised Common Lectionary. *Behold! Cultivating Attentiveness in the Season of Advent* is the second book of this set.

It is important, I believe, to tell a bit of the story about how *Simply Wait* came to be, because it is tied firmly to a wonderful spiritual practice that I learned many years ago. For those of you who have read *Simply Wait,* you may prefer to skip over the rest of this section, but if *Behold!* is your first experience of this book set, I encourage you to read the following description.

The idea for *Simply Wait* arose from my own experience with contemplative prayer, prayer that finds its home not in busy doing or speaking but in becoming, in being. Several years ago a friend suggested that we attend a one-day Advent retreat in which contemplative prayer played a part. I really did not have time to do this—especially during the busy season before Christmas, but my friend persisted and signed us up.

My friend and I experienced a spirit of quiet and calm the moment we arrived. The retreat meeting space did not overwhelm us with festive reds, greens, and golds; Christmas music did not greet us at the door. Instead, in the center of the room stood a small table draped with a plain purple cloth and adorned with a single burning candle. We were welcomed into a hospitable and generous silence. I still remember the stark impact of that space and silence. I had arrived out of breath from details of a Christmas that had not yet taken place.

In the course of that one day, a gracious convener led our small group through simple prayers, reading of Advent scriptures, and lots of quiet time in which to imagine how our life with God was being drawn toward Immanuel, God-With-Us. The activity that most stirred my imagination involved a spiritual exercise of simple attentiveness, attentiveness to a single word.

As retreat members sat in a circle, a basket filled with small pieces of folded paper came around. Each piece, we were told, had one word on it. Nothing more. The leader instructed us to take one, go to a quiet place in the building, and to sit with that word. We were to let our word sift through our thoughts and over our experiences as we contemplated what meaning it might hold in our life with God and our life with others. She urged us to take time with the word, allowing it to lead us into prayer and memories. We were given almost an hour to do so.

I recall my reaction to these instructions: *they could not be correct! How were we to spend so much time with one word? An article, maybe a paragraph, would be worth that much time, but not just a word.* We were a literate group, readers and thinkers, people who had taken time apart for this Advent day, and the leader wanted to use our valuable time with one single word?

But I followed the instructions, despite my suspicions of boredom or distraction related to whatever word I drew out of the basket. As our imposed quiet began, I slowly unfolded my little paper and saw the word in the palm of my hand: *Joy.* That was it. *Joy.* Over the next almost-hour, I found myself living with this word in ways that I could not have imagined had others not helped me make room for it that Advent day years ago. Songs came to mind, and faces came into view. Favorite times of day seemed to know the place of joy for me, as did certain childhood memories and vacation snapshots. I found myself wondering about the source of joy and why joy sometimes disappears in an instant. And, in all of this, my thoughts repeatedly returned to God. The time passed, and the prayers took form—all wrapped up in one little word and one short stretch of minutes spent with the One in whom my word had its home.

The pages of *Simply Wait* and *Behold!* offer you, either by yourself or in a group, some space in which to become attentive to words and to the Word. Not just any words will do here, but words chosen out of this most holy season of Advent. For each of the four weeks of this season, *a single word* has been discerned out of the scripture readings assigned for the week from the Revised Common Lectionary. Through a set of weekly guided spiritual practices, I invite you to live with an Advent word. Depending on the time you will have each week to use this resource, you may wish to follow all of the practices or to choose a few that most catch your Advent attention. The practices include the following:

- reflection
- silence
- prayer
- reading scripture
- reading or singing of hymn texts
- Christian service and action

For each week and word I describe a particular form of prayer from the Christian tradition. You may choose to learn or experience some new prayer practices. I selected these prayers for the way in which they illumine the word of the week and embody the word within our Advent living. Advent living is what Advent leads us toward: the Word embodied, Immanuel—"the Word became flesh and lived among us" (John 1:14).

I hope these prayers and practices will lead you to "behold," to attend to, your Advent way of life. May this book guide you through the season—one word at a time.

How to Use This Book

Participants

This book is designed for use by individuals, small groups, and classes.

Leaders

If you wish to use *Behold!* as a small-group resource, please refer to the Guide for Small Groups on page 99.

Time and Setting

The readings and exercises in this book are designed for daily use throughout the season of Advent, beginning on the first Sunday of Advent and ending on Christmas Eve. You may choose to read and reflect for a short time each day or to read the entire week's content in one longer period of time. Adapt the reading schedule to fit your Advent life. The time required to complete the reading and reflection for each day will vary from approximately ten minutes to thirty minutes, with the one exception being the prayer practices offered on Day Seven each week. To learn and practice these prayers will require different lengths and schedules of time. The prayer practices are also optional and can be set aside for use at another time of the year.

For individual reading time, choose a quiet space where you will face minimal interruption or distraction. The discipline of daily reading and reflection can be enhanced by keeping your reading material near a favorite seating area, having a candle to light before you begin (optional), and letting others around you know that you would like to have some quiet time.

Materials Needed

All you need to follow this resource is a personal copy of *Behold!*, a Bible (any translation), and something to write in, like a journal or notebook. As mentioned before, some persons find it helpful to light a candle before beginning to read.

Reading and Preparation

Behold! offers material for use during the four weeks of Advent, beginning, if at all possible, on the first Sunday of Advent and concluding with an invocation on Christmas Eve. The approximate time needed for each day's reading and reflection is as follows: Day One, 30 minutes; Days Two to Five, 10–15 minutes; Days Six and Seven, varies depending on the activity or prayer. Content may be read daily or in one or two slightly longer periods. If you choose to read all content for a week in one sitting, it will take approximately one hour to do so.

In each week's material you will find:

- Responding to a Word
  Each week begins with a single word that arises from the author's reading of the four scripture texts assigned for that week of Advent from the Revised Common Lectionary. Beginning on Day One with a time of guided silent reflection on the word, the remainder of the daily readings and exercises, including the selected prayer practice, also center on the chosen word. In addition, other prayers, scriptures, hymn texts, and a call to Christian action in the world illumine the word of the week in some way.

- Space for Making Notes or Journaling
  After each reading and reflection, the book's design provides open space to record notes, insights, drawings, prayers, and questions. Although you may prefer to use your own journal or notebook for this purpose, the open space in the book will help you keep your reflections close at hand and easy to find.

- Invocation and Silence
  A prayer of invocation can be found near the beginning of each week's content, followed by an invitation into silence. The author has discerned these opening prayers

through her own meditation on the word of the week. Consider praying these invocations on more than Day One; pray them daily if you can. If you do not have time on some days to do anything more than use these prayers and a time of silence, try to do so before you go to bed. Attending to a simple, daily prayer followed by silent prayer can become a way in which to behold the promises of God.

• Hymn to Read or Sing
An Advent hymn has been selected for each week, based upon the way its lyrics point to and illumine the word for the week. Whether you sing them or speak them, pay attention to the words of these songs as if you have never heard them before. Some may be unfamiliar to you, while you might know others by heart. Either way, behold their message and meaning once again.

• Benediction
Day One provides a weekly benediction that need not be limited to that one day. Consider using these blessings in your individual or group time or even in a congregational setting. Let these closing prayers send you out in peace.

• Reflections on the Word
Each week, following the readings and prayers for Day One, you are guided to the four Advent scripture texts designated in the Revised Common Lectionary. You may choose to read them all in one sitting, but they have been planned as individual daily readings. Note that you will be reading and reflecting on the texts *after* the Sunday in Advent for which they have been assigned, rather than in advance of their lectionary assignment. This intentional approach aids our attentiveness to these texts that can, when we hurry through them, be taken

for granted. By taking time with them after they have been read and proclaimed, we can behold their fullness in new ways.

After each scripture reading, a brief reflection is offered with questions and promptings for your own time of contemplation. Take your time with these. Permit the Holy Spirit to lead you through these opportunities to pay attention to the Word in slow and deliberate Advent ways.

- Weekly Advent Prayer Practice
  On Day Seven, you will find a brief introduction to a form of prayer that illumines some aspect of the word, the scripture (the Word), and reflections for that week. A guide to that selected prayer practice follows the introduction. None of these guides is an exhaustive or complete instruction manual for the practice. Additional resources are listed in the back of the book (page 103) should you desire more information. However, consider trying each of these prayers, alone or with a friend or group. Each requires a different amount of time; but all offer, in some unique way, help to attend to your relationship with God.

Before You Begin

Before you go farther in this book, I urge you to do all that you can to make room for the readings, prayers, and reflections that follow. Making room to be quiet, attentive, and still in the days that lead up to Christmas can be asking a lot. Most of us have become conditioned to the pressing schedules and seasonal distractions that seep into our calendars and surroundings, and Advent can be lost in a blurred and hurried holiday landscape. But, as best you can, try to find a setting where you can use this book for prayer and guidance so that you may grow in attentiveness to the One whose birth story we are about to recall and retell.

This is my hope for anyone who reads this book: that you will cultivate a deeper spiritual attentiveness to what matters to God about the gift of Jesus Christ; that you will begin and want to "see," to "behold," a bit differently than ever before. Perhaps you will grow to see and behold in the way author Esther de Waal so eloquently describes: "I want to see into the heart of a thing, to see beyond, to take time, to gaze. . . . I want the God-given way of seeing, not to possess and to control but to stand back in wonder and gratitude."[1]

Behold: may we all learn to see in wonder and gratitude this Advent season.

NOTES

1. Esther de Waal, "Attentiveness," *Weavings: A Journal of the Christian Spiritual Life*, XVII, no. 4 (July/August 2002): 23.

$\mathcal{A}$DVENT

WEEK ONE

EXPECTANCY

BEFORE YOU TURN THIS PAGE, pause silently for a moment.

Be alert to this one word: *Expectancy.*

Pay attention to your first response.

Let *expectancy* settle into your imagination and memory.

Do not hurry past the word.

Observe how it stirs up your senses—

sight, hearing, smell, touch, taste.

Attend to any stories it prompts from your life.

And when you have done so, turn the page.

Day One

ATTENDING TO THE WORD EXPECTANCY

What is your first response to this word?

How have you experienced *expectancy* in the past year?
Be as specific as possible. Take time with your memories.

What role has *expectancy* played in your spiritual life?
When and how has *expectancy* been significant
to your relationship with God?
Do not rush past these questions.
Stay with them for a while.

As you enter the season of Advent
and prepare for the celebration of Christmas,
how might God hope that you live in *expectancy*?
List particular ways in which
a posture of *expectancy* might help you behold
God's promise, Immanuel.

INVOCATION

O Expectancy,
born of fertile wonder,
belabored by narrowed hope;
craning curious lives forward,
drawing in the lonely and longing.
You are imagination's sister
and the brother of holy surprise.
Come, startle awake
our dozing apathy, our complacent dreams,
that we may behold your borning Advent cry.
Amen.

SILENCE

REFLECTION ON EXPECTANCY

For eleven months of every year, the small cardboard box was stored on the highest shelf of our hall closet. There it was out of my reach and practically hidden from my view by place mats, folded tablecloths, extra lightbulbs, and other household items in which I had no childhood interest. So that small brown box with its taped-up corners and slightly torn top remained safely out of sight and mind most of the time, collecting dust from January through November.

Then one late autumn day, the box would magically appear on the kitchen table—dust, tape, and all. When I close my eyes, I can still smell the mustiness of that aging cardboard and feel the brittle edges of the old tape that held the well-used box together. And without any effort at all, I recall the flush of excitement that warmed me from head to toe as soon as that little box was taken from the dark upper shelf and placed in front of me.

I could hardly wait to see what was inside—not because I did not know, but because I *did*. I knew what awaited me. I knew what I was looking forward to, what I was anticipating, what I was expecting. I knew because I had opened this box before and what it held grew no less exciting for me from one year to the next. As a matter of fact, my expectation seemed to increase as I grew older.

So slowly, with gentle hands, my mother would help me pull back the top flaps of the box, and there, in all their wonder were little piles of wrapped newspaper, worn dishrags, and tissue paper stacked on top of one another, filling the box from edge to edge. To the untrained eye, it seemed unremarkable, just a box of paper and rags. But I knew better! I knew what I would find there. And one by one, my mother would hand me and my sister and brother a swaddled treasure from that box, letting us unwrap it at our own pace.

A lamb. An angel. Joseph. A donkey. A shepherd. A wise man. Another lamb. Mary. On and on we would discover the beloved characters in our crèche, tossing aside the paper and cloth that had protected them for a year. We had learned what to look for. We had grown familiar with whom to expect. But the excitement and anticipation remained year after year, embedded in our expectancy, especially when one of us would find the small bundle that held baby Jesus, curled up and squirming in the brown cardboard trough fringed in a few pieces of glued straw.

And from that day until sometime after Christmas when my mother would quietly and carefully put the box back on that shelf, we could expect to find them all waiting for us on the coffee table in the living room. We would play with the figures, imagine with them, tell our own versions of the Christmas story; and they would play their part in the formation of our faith. All these years later. I still experience the same warming from head to toe when I bring a similar little brown box down from our attic sometime in late November. I expect to find the Christ child wrapped up in swaddling cloths and tissue paper and to behold the beauty of his birth through the season and, hopefully, beyond.

Hymn of Expectancy

Sing or read in unison the words of this Advent hymn. Attend to the words as though you have never heard them before.

Come, Thou Long-Expected Jesus

Come, thou long-expected Jesus,
born to set thy people free;
from our fears and sins release us,
let us find our rest in thee.
Israel's strength and consolation,
hope of all the earth thou art;
dear desire of every nation,
joy of every longing heart.

Born thy people to deliver,
born a child and yet a King,
born to reign in us forever,
now thy gracious kingdom bring.
By thine own eternal spirit
rule in all our hearts alone;
by thine all sufficient merit,
raise us to thy glorious throne.

Words: Charles Wesley, 1744.

BENEDICTION

May God's gracious presence wrap around and
    protect you.
May the promise of the holy Christ child
forever rest in the curve of your life.
May the sweet, fearless song of the Holy Spirit
sing you to sleep
and waken you in Advent dawns.
May you, and those you love and serve,
expect the good news,
Immanuel, God-With-Us.
Amen.

DAY TWO

READ ISAIAH 64:1-9

The people of God have fallen into a life pattern that no longer aligns with God's ways. They have neglected faithfulness; they have stopped calling on God's name. They have caved in to destructive distractions and selfish living and have chosen their own ways rather than God's ways. But they remember that God has been a saving force before, and they expect to find God waiting for them anyway. Instead, God seems absent.

So the people turn to the prophet Isaiah to plead their case before God. But notice where the prophet begins—it is not by telling God about the people. He begins, instead, by reminding the people about God. In other words, life with God is *first* about God and *then* about God's people.

It is not uncommon for us to approach the season of Advent with lists of our own expectations, as though the season begins and ends with us. So this year, let us enter the season by beholding and giving thanks for who God is and for what God has already done. Find a quiet place to sit in silence for at least five minutes. Think about the past year and identify four or five situations where God's grace surprised or encouraged you. Let each of these memories become an Advent prayer of thanksgiving.

Your reflections—

DAY THREE

READ PSALM 80:1-7, 17-19

"Restore us, O God;/ let your face shine, that we may be saved." Three times the psalmist punctuates the hymn with these words; three times he pleads for God to attend to the people's prayers—to end their suffering and tears, to recall past acts of mercy and liberation, to restore their lives once again in the face of oppressive enemies and leering neighbors. Would God's people sing such a song, repeat such a prayer if they did not expect God to hear their cries? Does this prayer not carry a deep, abiding note of expectancy despite what must have seemed to many a desperate and hopeless situation?

In the space below or in your journal, draw a circle large enough to write in the center the words, "Restore us, O God." Now, consider people and places in your life and God's world where there is a deep longing and need for restoration—physical, social, emotional, communal. List as many of these as you can around the edge of your circle, and when you have finished this exercise, offer an Advent prayer for restoration by reading the words in the center of the circle.

Your reflections—

DAY FOUR

READ 1 CORINTHIANS 1:3-9

"You are not lacking in any spiritual gift as you wait for the revealing of our Lord Jesus Christ." According to the apostle Paul, Christians have been given what we need in order to grow in faithfulness as we wait in expectancy for Christ to be revealed to us. We have what we need, not because of anything we do or own or accomplish, but because God faithfully provides the spiritual gifts required to become and live as people of faith. We are equipped to welcome, receive, follow, and serve the Lord Jesus Christ.

If you have a "Christmas list" begun where you list gifts you plan to give, take the list and at the top of it or in the margin, write down three "spiritual gifts" that God has already given you. Some examples might be patience, listening, prayer, compassion, wisdom, gentleness, teaching, faith, peace, healing, etc. Thank God for these gifts, and as the season moves forward, consider how you might share these gifts with others throughout the season.

Your reflections—

DAY FIVE

READ MARK 13:24-37

Expect the signs of the season, Jesus tells the disciples. Watch for tender shoots to appear on the branch; for leaves to unfurl. These words from Mark's Gospel point us to signs that we recognize but might have become so used to that we take them for granted. And yet, every time the fig tree bears fresh buds, they signal new beginnings and the passing away of the old.

What "signs" are taking place in the landscape around you? What is happening to the trees, flowers, sky, and earth where you live? When Advent begins, what changes are taking place in your part of the world? Make notes in the space below or in your journal. If you live in a different part of the world than when you were a child, take time to recall what changes you could expect to notice taking place in the Advent landscape and gardens of your childhood. Write an Advent prayer using some of these particular images and "signs" that God is at work and the kingdom is at hand.

Your reflections—

DAY SIX

BEHOLD THE WAITING WORLD

Who in your community would not expect to receive a kind word or offer of assistance from you? How might you, in a surprising way, extend the love of Immanuel, God-With-Us, to someone on the margin of the community in which you live? Consider where you might offer assistance in a personal way to someone who is sick, in prison, hungry, discouraged, in need, or in trouble. Resist pursuing an option that you would "expect" to do anyway, and challenge yourself to go where you would not usually expect to go. Let this Advent be a time of moving and responding beyond expectations in the spirit and love of Christ.

Your reflections—

DAY SEVEN

PRAYING IN EXPECTANCY

Praise the LORD, all you nations!
Extol him, all you peoples!
For great is his steadfast love toward us,
and the faithfulness of the LORD endures forever.
Praise the LORD!

—PSALM 117

PRAYING WITH IMAGES

Without knowing I was doing so, I have been praying with images from the time I could see. My parents filled our home with art, art books, and photography. I spent hours sitting beside my mother and father as they shared with me pages of prints by Degas, van Gogh, Renoir, Rembrandt, El Greco, and hundreds of others. We traveled to museums, cathedrals, parks, and city streets where sculpture, icons, and tapestries presented images that took my breath away even at a very young age. Only later, when I began to understand prayer, did I begin also to understand the ways in which visual images spark my prayer life to expect different contours of my soul and God's world to be revealed and experienced than when I pray with words. I need both. I need words, and I need images. I need to stimulate both sides of my brain and all parts of my heart. But only in the past few years have I become intentional about making room to pray with images as well as with words.

Advent is a particularly ripe time for learning to pray with images. Many paintings and scenes illumine some part of the Advent story: images of Mary and the angel Gabriel; drawings of Elizabeth and Mary greeting each other; paintings of Joseph and Mary headed to Bethlehem. There are starry nights, scenes of shepherds keeping their flocks, and rendering after rendering of the Holy Family on the night of Jesus' birth. Icons, crèches, art books, and illustrated Bibles all offer space for rich, wordless prayers that can guide us to expect the unexpected. In other words, using our eyes and imaginations with Advent imagery can help our prayer lives grow in expectancy that God is doing something new, revealing something new, touching something new in us and through us.

So I invite you to choose to pray with images this season, and offer the following guide to help you and others in this experience. May you have eyes to see with new Advent expectancy.

A Guide to the Practice of Praying with Images

Begin by selecting an image that illustrates some aspect of the Advent or Christmas story. Take your time with this selection. Look at art and photography books, online art resources, icons, family nativity scenes, library resources, magazines, and other sources of imagery. You may want to select a complex scene with many characters, or you may be drawn to a single figure or image. Trust your instinct and choose what catches your attention. You will have other opportunities to return to other images.

Once you have made your choice, take your image to a quiet place and get comfortable. You will want to give yourself at least twenty minutes for this prayer practice. Once you get settled, close your eyes for a few moments of silence and steady breathing. When you are ready, open your eyes and focus on the very first part of the image that catches your attention. Do your best to stay with this one part for a while. See it, look at it, really attend to it however small or insignificant to the whole image or figure it may seem at first—a tree, a hand, a halo.

After spending a few minutes with one part of your image, let your eyes take it all in. Take your time, noticing all that you can from one end to the other. Notice how you feel, what you think about, what stories or memories come to mind. Try not to edit your thoughts.

When the twenty minutes have passed, ponder these questions:

- What prayer arises in me as I focus on this image?
- For what or whom does this image prompt me to pray?
- Did God take me where I expected to go, or was there some element of surprise in my thoughts and prayers?

You may want to jot down your prayers and responses in a journal so that you can return to them another time. When you are finished, offer a silent prayer for this time.

Group Option: Share the instructions with others and ask them to bring their art choice with them, or you can provide a collection of images and figures from which each person can select one with which to pray after giving some time (10–15 minutes) for each person to choose.

After each person has made a selection, spend twenty minutes in silence in a comfortable posture and consider the questions above. After the time of silence, encourage each person to share his or her image and, if desired, to share any prayers and reflections. When all have finished, offer a silent prayer for this time together.

$\mathcal{A}$DVENT

WEEK TWO

PREPARATION

Before you turn this page, pause silently for a moment.

Be alert to this one word: *Preparation.*

Pay attention to your first response.

Let *preparation* settle into your imagination and memory.

Do not hurry past the word.

Observe how it stirs up your senses—

sight, hearing, smell, touch, taste.

Attend to any stories it prompts from your life.

And when you have done so, turn the page.

DAY ONE

ATTENDING TO THE WORD PREPARATION

What is your first response to this word?

How have you experienced *preparation* in the past year?
Be as specific as possible. Take time with your memories.

What role has *preparation* played in your spiritual life?
When and how has *preparation* been significant
to your relationship with God?
Do not rush past these questions.
Stay with them for a while.

As you live into the season of Advent and
anticipate the celebration of Christmas,
how might God hope that you prepare?
List particular ways in which an attitude of *preparation*
might help you behold
God's promise, Immanuel.

Invocation

Holy Preparation,
counterweight of surprise,
plumb line of hospitality;
you are fresh hay quickly strewn,
soft linen bands newly torn,
to hold the One who is to come.
O Preparation, catcher of the off guard,
leveler of all things high and low;
you are the smoother of rough edges
and bearer of good news.
Come, reveal our webs of apathy
with holy, sweeping light.
Amen.

Silence

Reflection on Preparation

I used to wonder why my great-aunt Lylla carefully prepared her beautiful flower gardens from spring through early fall, only to let them grow brown and scraggly in late autumn. For hours every day, as soon as small green stalks and leaves peeked through the springtime soil, she would weed, clear, and plant so that every bud and blossom had a chance for notice. Her dedicated garden work continued throughout the blooming season of summer into and beyond early fall. In my mind's eye, I can still see her, bent at the waist, circles of perspiration under the arms and down the back of her long cotton shirtwaist dress, hoe or rake in hand, and face hidden behind prolific, gloriously hued flower bushes. A frayed wicker tomato basket from the farmer's market sat near her feet, into which she would deftly toss weeds and cuttings from her work of preparing and tending the space she loved to spend time in.

Yet, when late autumn's colorful energy began to wind down, so too, it seemed, did Aunt Lylla's; her interest in preparing the garden for winter evaporated. It was as though, every year about that time, she just stopped caring about her garden. All that careful preparation of soil and space came to a screeching halt just when, in my childish point of view, it seemed to be most needed. Blooms, stalks, and stems dried out and shriveled; shiny green leaves turned brittle and gray. The cleared, well-groomed curves and lines of her garden began to be messy and unkempt, which was not my great-aunt's style in anything she did.

But what seemed odder still was that even with many of her flowers in ragged fragments on the ground—almost painful for me to look at—Aunt Lylla walked around her wilting, dying garden almost daily. She acted as though something was still happening there, something worth seeing and attending to. But all I could see was a sadly abandoned garden.

Only many years later did I learn the garden wisdom of my great-aunt. It took a while for me to understand what she knew about preparing a garden for the winter season. It took some time for me to discover what she had learned about "abandoning" the soil, space, and plants she spent so much time loving well from spring through autumn. She knew and was teaching me that it was God's season for working the garden. Aunt Lylla was turning over the preparation to God. Aunt Lylla was, in a deep way, abandoning the beauty and health of her garden to the One who first created it. My great-aunt had come to understand from a life of practice that while we could behold little above ground in the brittle, dying remnants of her garden as winter took its turn, plenty of life-giving growth, beauty, and change was taking place in the deep, dark earth below where we walked.

Aunt Lylla recognized that she shared the preparation of her garden—shared work between her and God, between creature and Creator. There was much to see through my great-aunt's eyes as she walked around the brown-gray stalks and fallen blossoms.

I had to learn to behold a different kind of beauty: the beauty of a garden at rest, a garden being restored, a garden waiting to become a new creation. God worked at preparing a new thing in the holy ground beneath us.

I shall be forever grateful to what Aunt Lylla taught me in her winter garden. And I pray that all of us learn to have eyes to behold the beauty of the Lord and hearts that trust God's steadfast preparing love.

Hymn of Preparation

Sing or read in unison the words of this Advent hymn. Attend to the words as though you have never heard them before.

Hail to the Lord's Anointed

Hail to the Lord's Anointed, great David's greater Son!
Hail in the time appointed, his reign on earth begun!
He comes to break oppression, to set the captive free;
to take away transgression, and rule in equity.

He comes with succor speedy to those who suffer wrong;
to help the poor and needy, and bid the weak be strong;
to give them songs for sighing, their darkness turn to light,
whose souls, condemned and dying, are precious in his sight.

He shall come down like showers upon the fruitful earth;
love, joy, and hope, like flowers, spring in his path to birth.
Before him, on the mountains, shall peace, the herald, go,
and righteousness, in fountains, from hill to valley flow.

To him shall prayer unceasing and daily vows ascend;
his kingdom still increasing, a kingdom without end.
The tide of time shall never his covenant remove;
his name shall stand forever; that name to us is love.

Words: James Montgomery, 1821 (Ps. 72)

BENEDICTION

A voice cries out in our wilderness:
"Prepare the way of the Lord:
soften your hearts;
heighten your hopes;
forge a way where there seems no way;
for Christ is coming to make all things new.
O people of God, prepare the way of the Lord!"
Amen.

Day Two

Read Isaiah 40:1-11

According to the prophet's warning, radical landscape changes must take place to prepare the way of the Lord. Crooked highways will be straightened; low places will be lifted and high places lowered; what is uneven will be no longer be so. The way of the Lord will become a level path for all who choose to follow. But notice that the scripture says nothing about its becoming an easier way to go—not for the Lord or for anyone else. It is just radically different and changed; it still goes through wilderness, desert, valley, plain, and unfamiliar territory.

In these early Advent days, allow the prophet's words to guide you. Meditate on this scripture text. What gets in the way, what obstructs your ability to accept God's invitation to follow Jesus? In the space below, name some obstacles in your spiritual life. What seems too high, too low, too hard, too unclear about your journey of faith? Be as specific as possible and list what comes to mind. Then prayerfully ask for and imagine God's help to prepare a way of the Lord in your Advent life.

Your reflections—

DAY THREE

READ PSALM 85:1-2, 8-13

Settle into a quiet place where you can read aloud these verses
from Psalm 85, a psalm most often read at Advent because of its
clear portrayal of God's promised return, which will bring peace
and restoration to the people, even in the midst of their present
brokenness. Read the verses once. Sit in silence for a minute, then
slowly read the verses a second time.

Now focus on verse 13: "Righteousness will go before him,
and will make a path for his steps." Sketch a path in the space
below from one corner to another. Make it as straight or curv-
ing as you choose. Then mark the path with three "stepping-
stones"—one at the beginning, one in the middle, and one at the
end—each large enough for you to write one word in the center.
Go back to the verses in the psalm and choose three words that
catch your attention. Do not overthink your choices; just receive
them. Write each word across one of the path's stones. Prepare a
place in your prayers for these three words and offer each to God
for whatever reason it has caught your attention.

Your reflections—

DAY FOUR

READ 2 PETER 3:8-15A

While the people of God wait for the promised return of the Lord, this epistle urges them to prepare by living "lives of holiness and godliness." As you consider this instruction given to the early Christian community, think about people in your life—past and present—whose lives, in some way, evidenced what you might describe as holiness or godliness. Make a list of ten people, and beside each name write a brief description (a word or two will do) about why you placed him or her on this list. What attributes, commitments, qualities, or experiences brought this person to mind? Do not rush through the list; let your memory stretch back to ponder the many people you have known.

When you have completed the list, consider writing a note of gratitude and encouragement to at least one of these persons or to one of their family members as a way to prepare your life for Advent living.

Your reflections—

DAY FIVE

~

READ MARK 1:1-8

Mark's Gospel begins with the appearance of Jesus' cousin, John the baptizer. John, sent by God, prepares the way for Jesus' earthly ministry. John's preparation for the Lord is made known by what he says and proclaims, what he does and does not do, and who he is and who he knows he is not. John is not the Messiah; he comes to prepare the way for the One who is.

Take some time to reflect on persons you know who are younger than you, who are from generations after yours: children, youth, young adults. In what ways do you live out your faith in Jesus Christ that bears witness to these next generations? How do their lives and your life intersect in the body of Christ and in the world in ways that encourage you to "prepare the way of the Lord" for them? Think about how, in these Advent and Christmas seasons, you can be present to other generations through prayers, presence, gifts, service, and witness. Record three specific actions you can take to help prepare the way for those who follow in your footsteps of faith.

Your reflections—

DAY SIX

BEHOLD THE WAITING WORLD

Where in your community has room been prepared tonight for a homeless family to come in off the street? What steps must be taken to prepare this place for them—for their food, hygiene, safety, bedding? What qualifications must the family meet to use this space? Would any family be turned away and, if so, for what reasons?

If you are already involved with a community shelter for homeless guests, take this time to learn all you can about what is involved in preparing to house the guests. Meet with the director or pastor and pay attention to the details. If you are not yet involved, find out how the way is prepared for the homeless who come to your town to find a safe place for a night or more. Then prayerfully consider your involvement in the preparations needed during this Advent season and beyond.

Your reflections—

DAY SEVEN

PRAYING IN PREPARATION

For God alone my soul waits in silence,
for my hope is from him.

—PSALM 62:5

SILENT PRAYER

Few prayer practices have been as life-altering for me as silent prayer. To pray in silence, even if momentary, affirms that prayer begins with God. Silent prayer requires that we stop talking and feeling solely responsible for the content of our communication with God and that, instead, we trust that God has something for us to receive and that God will meet us in prayer—is waiting for us in prayer—whether or not we know how to pray in the moment. For people of faith "from the beginning of time, and in all religions, God has been associated with eternal silence."[1]

To enter a time of silent prayer implies that we intentionally make room within us to *listen for God.* Many of us find this silent listening difficult to do because we have become accustomed to the sound of our own voice, culture, and ambient noise that surround us. Silence may stir up impatience, awkwardness, and self-consciousness. For others, waiting for God in silence is like slipping into a refreshing pool of water on a warm day; it is easy and soothing. Either way, difficult or easy, I have found that intentional silent prayer opens space in our souls that for myriad reasons we have closed off, hurried around, or never intentionally opened before God. I have also discovered that silent prayer brings out the dreamer, the worrier, the confessor, and the prodigal in us and does so in ways of intimacy, honesty, and mystery that are not always accessible without making room for God in silence. Consider the lives of Elizabeth and Zechariah, Mary and Joseph. Each of them, alone with God, received guidance toward a deeper life of faith and trust. Perhaps their stories can help us perceive Advent as an especially ripe time to cultivate silent prayer in God's presence.

Silent prayer offers no form to follow but our own—one of its many gifts. We are completely free to be in touch with God in any way and about any matter. It also seems to me that silent prayer heightens our awareness that God's prayers for us are as active as are our prayers to God; silent prayer illumines a holy mutuality. Even if our minds race, even if our prayers play on fast-forward or sometimes seem invisible or absent, intentional silent time with God creates room in our hearts for God's voice to be as present in prayer as our own. Silence prepares a place like no other to meet God-With-Us, breath to breath and heart to heart, whether for a moment, ten minutes, an hour, or more.

So let us join Zechariah and Mary and the others in our Advent story and learn to wait upon and behold the Lord in silent time. Let us practice with intent, coming into the presence of our Creator, our God, the Holy One, to be still, to be present, and to be who we are—God's beloved.

A GUIDE TO THE PRACTICE OF SILENT PRAYER

Two lessons about silence have most helped me grow in its practice as a way of prayer.

Silence is the quality of stillness within and around oneself.[2]

Silence is "fasting from speech, not absence of sound."[3]

Each statement affirms what I have experienced through this form of prayer: that silence exists as one of God's many gifts. We do not create silence—we seek, enter, and make room for it; but God makes it available to us anytime, even in the noisiness and activity of life. We can become silent anywhere, just as we can commune with God anywhere. This availability, however, does not mean that silence comes easily for us. It does not mean that most of us find silence as a simple way to pray. Rather, some have suggested that silent prayer is the "hardest of all . . . because most of us are so unused to silence, to waiting, to being still and feeling our souls become still."[4]

The instructions for this practice acknowledge this possibility—that the practice of silent prayer involves more and requires more than simply becoming still and quiet. They try to honor the teachings of many spiritual guides and saints of the past: the practice of silent prayer, like any practice, requires intent, preparation, and discipline in order to become fully our own. The guide on the next pages may be one you choose to employ in a regular practice of silent prayer, but other models and traditions are available for your exploration. Also, this practice is designed for use in solitude or in a group setting.

Silent prayer is a prayer for any time of day or night. For the purpose of this guide, choose a time of day when you can have at least twenty minutes of dedicated silence, remembering that silence is about your not speaking, not necessarily about your being in a quiet place. Choose your place for prayer based on where you can be most intentional about having uninterrupted silence. You may need to let others around you know about your undertaking and tell them that they need not tiptoe; rather, they need to go about their lives. This, in part, is the discipline of silent prayer: we learn to practice it wherever we choose to be.

You may want to set an alarm for the twenty-minute period, so that you know when the time is complete should you choose to close your eyes during the prayer. In time, you may wish to extend or shorten your silent prayers. There is no right or wrong length of time for this practice. An intentional minute with God in silence can offer far more than we might imagine based on our understanding of time.

- Select the day, time, and place you will pray in silence. If desired, set an alarm for a twenty-minute period. (This time can vary according to your schedule or desire.)

- Settle into the place however you choose—sit, lie down, kneel, walk. Close your eyes if it helps you to focus on why you are here: to be with God, to come before God.

- Breathe deeply, finding a rhythm of breath that feels comfortable. Remember that God is both as close as your breath and the source of your breath. *Ruach*, breath, Holy Spirit, will be with you and help you draw close to the One who waits to meet you in the silence.

- Enter into the silence by listening to all that is present when you stop speaking. What sounds are around you? Do not be concerned about the distractions of the sounds. In time, the more you practice silence, they will become less noticeable.

- Thank God in whatever way you choose for being with you in this time. Imagine yourself coming before God. Wait for God, place your life and worries and hopes before God. Place the needs of the world before God, trusting that God's desires for the world are already present too.

- Wait in silence. As distracting thoughts come to you, be patient and gentle with yourself about them, try to put them aside, breathe deeply, and remain silent before God. Practice waiting, even if it seems that nothing is happening.

- Wait for God and listen. Breathe.

- Offer to God what is on your mind and heart, what is heavy and light in your soul. Ask God anything, any questions, even about distractions that arise. Listen for

God's presence, trusting that what matters to you matters to God and that what matters to God is being shared with you.

- Wait and listen. Again, even if it seems that nothing is happening, trust that something very important is at work: you are honoring God with every part of your being; you are doing nothing but being present to God and listening.

- Whisper "Amen," and gently release yourself from silence when your prayer time is over,.

Optional: If you choose to practice silent prayer in a group, you may wish to add a brief time of conversation after the prayers are completed. Or, if you use a journal, you could individually or communally take a time of response. Some questions might include the following:

- How did you experience the silence today?

- What did this silence tell you about God?

- What did this silence tell you about yourself?

- What response did the silence call for from you?

NOTES

1.   John Killinger, *Beginning Prayer* (Nashville, TN: Upper Room Books, 1993), 38.
2.   Rueben P. Job and Norman Shawchuck, *A Guide to Prayer for All God's People* (Nashville, TN: Upper Room Books, 1990), 17.
3.   Gwen White, in a presentation on "Solitude and Silence" during "Retreat Leadership Training" by The Upper Room and Scarritt-Bennett Center, Nashville, TN, February 1995.
4.   Killinger, *Beginning Prayer*, 38.

$\mathscr{A}$DVENT

WEEK THREE

FAITH

Before you turn this page, pause silently for a moment.

Be alert to this one word: *Faith*.

Pay attention to your first response.

Let *faith* settle into your imagination and memory.

Do not hurry past the word.

Observe how it stirs up your senses—

sight, hearing, smell, touch, taste.

Attend to any stories it prompts from your life.

And when you have done so, turn the page.

DAY ONE

─⁓─

ATTENDING TO THE WORD FAITH

What is your first response to this word?

How have you experienced *faith* in the past year?
Be as specific as possible. Take time with your memories.

What role has *faith* played in your spiritual life?
When and how has *faith* been significant
to your relationship with God?
Do not rush past these questions.
Stay with them for while.

As you live into the season of Advent
and prepare for the celebration of Christmas,
how would you describe the shape of your *faith* to God?
List particular ways in which attentiveness to *faith*
might help you behold God's promise, Immanuel.

INVOCATION

O Faith,
as visible as stardust,
as unseen as dusk at dawn;
as strong as the force of gravity,
as vulnerable as the power of love;
you are the veil of light behind closed eyes,
the heart's anchor beneath waves of doubt.
Come, reveal yourself like shadow to candlelight,
loom large, draw near,
as we find our Advent way.
Amen.

SILENCE

REFLECTION ON FAITH

There was a stream at the edge of my grandparents' yard. For all
the years that I played in it, sat near it, escaped to it, and walked
beside it, I have never known where it begins or ends, nor have
I felt the need to know. It is deep enough to wade in, to hold
fascinating little water creatures; and it is safe enough to have
navigated and explored since I was a little girl. I have experienced
this stream as a source of power, beauty, mystery, and goodness
in every season of my life. And, in every season, I have learned
something from the stream about the One who created it; I have,
especially, learned much about faith.

The stream has been on my grandparents' land since before it
was their land. It holds fossils and shells from past currents, times,
and generations. The stream still runs through that land, even
though my grandmother and grandfather are no longer living. In
long Alabama droughts, it adapted, sometimes becoming cracked,
muddy earth but never losing its shape, purpose, or readiness to

fill to the brim when the rains came. When those pelting rains did come, the usually lazy water could flash over the banks in less time than it took me to run up the hill to the screen porch where my grandmother waited with a warm, dry towel. And whether as slimy clay-mud or minnow-laden water, the stream always has something to offer and teach anyone willing to pay attention to it. Even as a young child, I somehow knew that what appeared narrow enough to leap across and shallow enough to stand in was at the same time bigger and deeper and longer than anything I could see with my own two eyes.

Enduring much stirring up and resistance through the years—every childhood attempt to obstruct it, change its direction, and even pollute it—this stream always clears and returns faithfully to its created way and path. On some summer evenings, my cousins and I left a dam of rocks, bricks, leaves, and bottles packed down into the clay as hard as we could pack them, certain that we could change the stream overnight into a hip-deep wading pool. But each morning, we would awaken to find remnants of our big muddy work pushed aside by that tenacious flow of water that seemed so much smaller to us than what we had put in its way. The stream pressed everything firmly to the side, and rolled on through. We did not detour its mission for long. We could either be part of it or try to thwart it.

In time, I stopped trying to change the stream. Instead, I began to pay closer attention to it, to live with it as it was, to respect it. The more I matured, the more I valued that stream in deep, new ways of rest, play, and imagination.

Whenever I return to my grandparents' land, I walk down the hill to the stream. In recent years, I have taken my own family to its banks where we have played, dreamed, and waded. I want to share the stream with the people I love, in the same way it was shared with me for all of these years. I can rarely resist standing barefoot in its water or searching for the fascinating, intricate life-forms that make their home in its mud, rocks, and water. Looking back now, I see that spending time in the stream was never about me changing it; it was always about me being changed.

I love this stream, and as much as its curves and banks have held and carried my life through many seasons, I also hold and carry it in the contours of my inner life. In this way the stream on my grandparents' land reveals much to me about faith, about the flow and form of what I have come to believe.

So in this Advent season, I pray that all of us look to the source of living water that is never far away but in fact runs through the course of our lives. May we grow in attentiveness to the faithful ways of God that surround, guide, and change us if we will have eyes and hearts to see.

HYMN OF FAITH

Sing or read in unison the words of this Advent hymn. Attend to the words as though you have never seen or heard them before.

My Soul Gives Glory to My God

My soul gives glory to my God.
My heart pours out its praise.
God lifted up my lowliness
in many marvelous ways.

My God has done great things for me:
yes, holy is this name.
All people will declare me blessed,
and blessings they shall claim.

From age to age, to all who fear,
such mercy love imparts,
dispensing justice far and near,
dismissing selfish hearts.

Love casts the mighty from their thrones,
promotes the insecure,
leaves hungry spirits satisfied,
the rich seem suddenly poor.

Praise God, whose loving covenant
supports those in distress,
remembering past promises
with present faithfulness.

Words by Miriam Therese Winter
© Copyright Medical Mission Sisters, 1978, 1987

BENEDICTION

There was a man sent from God whose name was John.
He came as a witness to testify to the light,
but he himself was not the light.
The true light, which enlightens everyone,
is coming into the world.
The true light, by which all things come into being,
is the light of the world.
The light shines in the darkness,
and the darkness will not overcome it.
Behold! Our God comes to us
that we may reflect the light of love on earth.
Amen.

DAY TWO

READ ISAIAH 61:1-4, 8-11

Advent is a season of good news. In this season we prepare, by faith, to celebrate the birth of God-With-Us, Immanuel. According to the prophet Isaiah, this good news comes not just for us whose lives have been attuned to listen for, celebrate, and receive it; it comes also for the many others who wait day and night for us to act upon it—the oppressed; the brokenhearted; the captives and prisoners; the mourning, ruined, and devastated.

If we pay attention to world news, we cannot claim ignorance about the great need for the good news of Jesus Christ to break into the world. In the space below, create a list of the following categories, leaving room beside each one to make a note: oppressed, broken-hearted, prisoners, mourning, ruined, devastated. Using any news source, name a place in the world where people live in the shadow and circumstance of each category. If you are unfamiliar with the details of the situation, become familiar sometime this week and include these persons and situations in your prayers. If your prayers lead you toward action, ask God to guide you in the name and spirit of Christ.

Your reflections—

DAY THREE

READ PSALM 126

In many ways, Advent is a "not yet" season. Mary and Joseph have *not yet* traveled to Bethlehem, the infant Jesus has *not yet* been born, the angels have *not yet* appeared to the shepherds, and the star has *not yet* come to rest over the manger. Still, with all these "not yets" embedded in the Advent story, we spend these days and weeks living in faith that God will provide what has been promised—a long-awaited Messiah, a living hope.

Psalm 126 is also about a "not yet" time in the lives of God's people. They are in exile, removed from the familiar, joyful, fruitful lives they once had. And although they are in a season where there is not yet laughter, not yet joy, not yet fruitful harvest, they take time to remember, dream about, and share faith in God whom they believe hears their prayers.

Consider this concept of "not yet" and carry it in imagination to the city, town, or village in which you live. Where is there "not yet" enough for some children to eat, a place for the homeless to live, some afternoon company for a lonely person to receive? Where is there "not yet" needed leadership in your faith community or needed volunteers in your local community? How might your faith lead you to bring hope to one "not yet" circumstance so that you share in God's restoring Advent love? Select one such situation in your community, and describe in the space below what you could do in the name of love.

Your reflections—

DAY FOUR

READ 1 THESSALONIANS 5:16-24

We may feel the burden of faith when reading these verses from First Thessalonians. Rejoice, give thanks, and pray *always*. Hold fast to what is good and resist *all* evil. How often do these instructions become heavy and, if we are honest with one another, seem impossible? Being a faithful follower of Jesus is not easy, not in Advent, not at Christmas, not anytime. Christian faith asks much of us. The list of spiritual goals and desired qualities of the faithful Christian life stretches out around us, often appearing beyond our reach.

But for a moment, take time to immerse yourself in verse 24 of today's reading: "The one who calls you is faithful." Read this verse again. Now ponder for a few silent moments the significance of these words. God who calls you to faith is faithful. God is with you, will be faithful to you, and is working a good work in your life right now.

Recall from this past week one time when you sensed God's faithful presence. Note the specifics of this memory: Where were you? Who was with you? What was taking place? What were you feeling? After you have spent time with this memory, offer a prayer of thanksgiving to God.

Your reflections—

Day Five

READ JOHN 1:6-8, 19-28

John the baptizer was not the Messiah. He was not the one the people were looking for; he was not "the light." But he was sent as a witness to the light and to testify that God's people must have faith that the light, the "one who is coming," was about to enter into their lives in world-changing ways.

Looking back through your life and Advent seasons of the past, how have you been reminded that Christmas was coming? What symbols, traditions, scriptures, stories, songs, or other signs did your family and community use to "witness" to and shed "light" on the celebration of Christmas? Make a list of five favorite symbols, traditions, or activities; then take time to recall and describe what each represented to you about the coming of Christ. Note any new insight about what now serves as a "witness" to the light of Christ for you through Advent symbols, liturgy, actions, or in other ways.

Your reflections—

DAY SIX

BEHOLD THE WAITING WORLD

This week commit to become more attentive to world news. Choose a source [online, TV/radio, print] for this news, and be intentional about looking for news stories from countries and continents other than your own. From a faith perspective, note what is taking place for God's people around the world, especially those in need of assistance, compassion, and justice. Let your faith guide you to choose one particular story and to become engaged in a personal way of your choosing with a brother or sister represented by the story. Consider this an Advent spiritual discipline, a witness of faith. If you are not familiar with the location of the story, prayerfully find out about it so that you can begin to pay attention to the place in God's world to which you are now connected with new insight.

Your reflections—

DAY SEVEN

PRAYING IN FAITH

I love the LORD, because he has heard
my voice and my supplications.
Because he inclined his ear to me,
therefore I will call on him as long as I live.

—PSALM 116:1-2

USING PRAYER BEADS

Several years ago a good friend gave me a simple wooden rosary. He had grown up in the Roman Catholic church and had always welcomed my questions and interest about spiritual-life practices of his tradition. He had taught me about prayer cards, Benedictine spirituality, the sign of the cross, and many other meaningful influences on his rich prayer life. When I asked him about his experience with rosaries, he shared some of his childhood and family history of the prayer practice and then described the prayers he had learned. Weeks later, a small envelope was dropped off for me at my office. No accompanying note identified the sender. When I opened it, I found a rosary and knew the source. The rosary was beautiful: light wooden beads connected by dark brown cord stretched and knotted in a clear pattern, with a small wooden and metal crucifix hanging at the end.

I had never owned a rosary before. In fact, growing up in the Protestant tradition in America, I had been taught that prayer beads of any kind were not to be used, along with icons, statues, and most sensory aids to prayer. In my personal experience in the church, praying with beads has been continued only by Roman Catholic and some Orthodox communities. But in recent years many different streams of Protestant Christianity are recovering the contemplative use of prayer beads, a recovery for which I am deeply grateful. I have always been intrigued, from a distance, as I watch others touch, hold, and pray with the beads. I am a tactile and kinesthetic learner—drawn to texture, shape, and movement. I find that the sense of touch allows me to slow down and keeps me focused in ways that words sometimes fail me. So the first private moment I had with that beautiful rosary, I could hardly wait to hold and feel the beads between my fingers.

With no compulsion to pray in a particular way, I first held the cross, then began to move from bead to bead. As I did, the names of family and friends came to mind. One bead, one name; another bead, another name; and I was praying. And in that first time, I was aware that my focus was different, as if the feel of the bead and the clarity of where to go next physically held my attention more fully than when I process my prayers by thought alone. Each bead prompted a name and engaged my prayer memory for people I carried in my heart. But because my body, through my fingers, was involved, I felt fully present to the prayers—body, mind, and spirit—in a way that I had not felt before.

In the years since receiving that first rosary, I have developed a personal form of daily prayer in which I use prayer beads. The guide that I offer is only one of many guides that are available. Several prayer bead resources are listed ion pages 103–104 of this book, including online sources to purchase prayer beads.

Advent is a season in which many of us already use the senses of sight, smell, hearing, taste, and touch to heighten and deepen our worship and spiritual life experiences. May you be open to the added prayer practice of using prayer beads, an ancient and holy way to contemplate life with God and one another.

A GUIDE TO THE PRACTICE OF USING PRAYER BEADS

Plan for at least twenty minutes of prayer time. Choose a location that provides an atmosphere and attitude of quietness, whether you are alone or in a group. Prayer beads offer a contemplative practice for individuals and for groups. You will need two items: a set of prayer beads and a prayer pattern to guide your prayers. You may purchase prayer beads from many sources, or you may choose to make a set. The Resources section of this book (pages 103–104) gives more information about how to purchase or make prayer beads. The designs of prayer beads will vary in size, number, and symbolism. For the purpose of this book, I refer to Anglican prayer beads (see page 76), which incorporate thirty-three beads and a cross, but you may choose to use a different design and adapt the prayer pattern accordingly.

For the pattern of prayer offered here, I use the following four intercessory categories found in Rueben P. Job's book *When You Pray: Daily Practices for Prayerful Living*. Those categories are as follows: (1) Prayer for the World, Its People, and Leaders; (2) Prayer for the Church and Its Leaders; (3) Prayer for Those in Our Circle of Responsibility; and (4) Prayer for Ourselves.[1] Feel free to use any prayer categories that help you pray.

Use these symbols to guide you through the prayer pattern that follows:

✠   Cross

●   Week beads (Intercessory beads)

●   Cruciform beads (Jesus Prayer beads)

○   Invitatory bead (Lord's Prayer bead)

NOTES

1.   Rueben P. Job, *When You Pray: Daily Practices for Prayerful Living* (Nashville, TN: Abingdon Press, 2009), 23.

Anglican Prayer Beads

Week Three

Pattern of Prayer Using Prayer Beads

- Begin with the cross, holding it in one hand and giving praise to God for this time of prayer.

- Then move to the Invitatory bead, and offer a prayer of gratitude and praise as a call to prayer.

- Next, move to the first Cruciform bead, and here and each time you come to another Cruciform bead, offer the Jesus Prayer: "Lord Jesus Christ, have mercy on me."

- As you move from a Cruciform bead to the first and following Intercessory beads, offer any intercessory prayers that come to you by name, one bead at a time. Use the intercessory categories listed on page 74 to guide you, beginning with: "Prayer for the World, Its People, and Leaders." As you recall world events, name prayer needs one by one as you move from bead to bead. It may take you many beads to work through one intercessory category, but just keep moving along the circle until you are ready for the next intercessory category: "Prayer for the Church and Its Leaders." Follow the same pattern through each intercessory category—"Prayer for Those in Our Circle of Responsibility," "Prayer for Ourselves." Whenever you come to a Cruciform bead, stop and offer the Jesus Prayer, then return to your intercessions. Your prayers may lead you around the prayer bead circle several times or only once. When you have completed your intercessions:

- Return to the Invitatory bead and offer the Lord's Prayer.

- Finally, hold the cross and pray, "Amen."

$\mathcal{A}$DVENT

WEEK FOUR

Promise

BEFORE YOU TURN THIS PAGE, pause silently for a moment.

Be alert to this one word: *Promise.*

Pay attention to your first response.

Let *promise* settle into your imagination and memory.

Do not hurry past the word.

Observe how it stirs up your senses—

sight, hearing, smell, touch, taste.

Attend to any stories it prompts from your life.

And when you have done so, turn the page.

DAY ONE

ATTENDING TO THE WORD PROMISE

What is your first response to this word?

How have you experienced *promise* in the past year?
Be as specific as possible. Take time with your memories.

What role has *promise* played in your spiritual life?
When and how has *promise* been significant
to your relationship with God?
Do not rush past these questions.
Stay with them for a while.

As you live into the season of Advent
and prepare for the celebration of Christmas,
how might *promise* enter into your life
with God, neighbor, and creation?
List particular ways in which God's promise,
Immanuel, God-With-Us,
has influenced how you live your life.

Holy Promise,
glistening thread on the prophet's loom;
weaving frayed remnants of what has been
into fresh textures of what can be.
Over you some hearts are crossed;
because of you some hearts are broken.
Mending, stretching, hemming, creating:
swaddling bands, garment fringe, linen cloths.
Come, slip around and not through
our waiting hope,
that we may be bound to you now and in every season.
Amen.

SILENCE

REFLECTION ON PROMISE

"I am with you."

Words of a promise—a promise most remembered from another season and another place—not at Christmas near Bethlehem but at Easter in Galilee. "I am with you always," the resurrected Jesus promises the eleven remaining disciples at the end of Matthew's Gospel, as they stand waiting for a word from him about what to do next (28:20).

But this same promise resounds as the promise of Advent, for the story of Christmas rests on it. "I am with you," God promises the people of Israel through the words of the prophets and psalmists (2 Sam. 7:13; Ps. 23; Ps. 100; Isa. 43). Though the people betray God and turn their backs, though they sin and follow other gods time and time again, still God promises through different voices and in different ways, "I am with you."

"I am with you," God promises Mary through the angel Gabriel (Luke 1:28, AP). "I am with you and find favor with you. I have chosen you to be with me by the power of the Holy Spirit." Then Mary replies, "I promise to be with you according to your word. Yes, I am with you, God" (Luke 1:38, AP). No matter what comes or where she must go or what she must endure, Mary, against all human logic, promises to be with God. She agrees to the out-of-the blue request for the sake of the world's future.

"I am with you," God promises Joseph, Mary's husband-to-be, in a dream. "I am with you now and I will be with you soon in the form of the child you will name Jesus. I know you are afraid but don't be. I am with you" (Matt. 1:20-23, AP). So wherever Joseph must now go, whatever he must now do, he has the promise that God-With-Us, Immanuel, is already with him.

"I am with you," Joseph promises Mary (Matt. 1:24, AP). That promise makes no social sense and has no cultural value. It could be a very dangerous promise. An upright man takes as his wife a girl already pregnant with someone else's child? Who could expect him to keep this promise? "I am with you, Mary," Joseph whispers to her; "I am not afraid to take you as my wife for God is with us both."

Promise by promise, the Advent story stretches out, like bands of cloth across a waiting manger. "I am with you," God promises, through the words of prophets; in the songs of psalmists; from the lips of angels; by a fresh, tiny birth cry in the night. And intersecting each strand of promise made by God, another promise is placed: from the yes of a girl, by the trust of a man, through the hope of a people, in the flesh of humanity. From the beginning to the end, Jesus Christ embodies God's promise to the world, for you and for me: "I am with you."

May each of us this Advent not take this promise lightly. As we approach the manger in Bethlehem, may we carry a strand of promise from our life and offer it as a gift to the newborn King, God's promise-with-us, now and always.

Hymn of Promise

Sing or read in unison the words of this Advent hymn. Attend to the words as though you have never heard them before.

Lo, How a Rose E'er Blooming

Lo, how a Rose e'er blooming from tender stem hath sprung!
Of Jesse's lineage coming, as those of old have sung.
It came, a floweret bright, amid the cold of winter,
when half spent was the night.

Isaiah 'twas foretold it, the Rose I have in mind;
with Mary we behold it, the Virgin Mother kind.
To show God's love aright, she bore to us a Savior,
when half spent was the night.

O Flower, whose fragrance tender with sweetness fills the air,
dispel in glorious splendor the darkness everywhere.
True man yet very God, from sin and death now save us,
and share our every load.

Sts. 1–2, 15th cent. German; trans. Theodore Baker; st. 3 from *The Hymnal*, 1940
St. 3 © 1940, 1943, renewed 1971 The Church Pension Fund

Benediction

Behold, people of God,
the promise is given!
A cry in the wilderness;
a babe in the night;
a star in the sky
a Savior for the world.
Hear, listen, and see
that the Lord is very near!
Amen and Amen.

DAY TWO

READ 2 SAMUEL 7:1-11, 16

Here, deeply embedded in the Old Testament story about King David and the prophet Nathan, comes a new word about God's promise to the people of Israel. Not only does God promise that David will become a great name, that the people of Israel will be given a place to live, and that David will receive rest from his enemies; but through Nathan's prophecy, God extends the promise to David that a house and lineage will be established "forever." From this time forward, the relationship between God and David's descendants, between God and the people of Israel, will be one of never-ending unconditional grace. Nothing will separate the people of Israel from God's steadfast love. This is now God's promise, unconditional and forever.

In the space below, write these words from the scripture text: "God's steadfast love will not be taken from me." Reflect on the following questions: *What does steadfast love mean to me? What does it look like? What does it feel like? To whom have I made this promise to offer steadfast love?*

Now hold in prayer these persons to whom you have promised steadfast love.

Your reflections—

DAY THREE

❧

READ LUKE 1:47-55

In verses 54-55 of Mary's song, she sings, "He has helped his servant Israel, in remembrance of his mercy, according to the promise he made to our ancestors, to Abraham and to his descendants
forever." As a young girl, Mary knew the promises that God had
made to her people. Somewhere early in her life, Mary learned
about God and God's ways. She had taken the scriptures of her
people to heart and as a youth could sing about and witness to
God's promises.

When you were a youth, did you participate in a community of faith? If so, recall some of the people and activities that
most influenced your spiritual life. Be specific, and use the space
below to list these if you wish. If you did not participate in a
community of faith in your teenage years, recall persons and
circumstances that, during those years, influenced your faith in
other settings. When you have spent time with these recollec-
tions, offer a prayer of gratitude for the ways in which God's
promises have been made known to you.

Your reflections—

DAY FOUR

READ ROMANS 16:25-27

In these closing verses of the letter to the Romans, Paul praises God for the mystery of faith made known in Jesus Christ. In Jesus, God is revealed, accessible, and present in ways that were "kept secret for long ages." Jesus' birth in the city of David in Bethlehem revealed God to all people, Immanuel, God-With-Us. All came about just as God had promised "through the prophetic writings."

Prayerfully ask yourself: *In the past year, since last Christmas, where has Christ been made known to me? Where have I witnessed the love of Christ in my life? Where have I witnessed the love of Christ in the world?* As situations, images, or stories come to mind, jot them down in the space below. Then, in the name and power of Jesus Christ, offer a prayer of gratitude.

Your reflections—

DAY FIVE

READ LUKE 1:26-38

In these verses, God's messenger, the angel Gabriel, astounds an unsuspecting Mary. Gabriel's news catches the young girl off guard. She is going about her predictable life in an everyday way. She will soon become the wife of a local man and live according to local custom. But a few perplexing words interrupt her routine and confront her with a decision of overwhelming magnitude. She must have time to ponder what she hears. She needs time to consider, as best a young girl can, what a yes or a no could mean.

And somewhere between the angel's appearance and departure, between what we have as verses 26 and 38, Mary makes her choice. Mary chooses yes and makes a promise to God that turns her life and our lives completely upside down.

Often, we get so caught up in Mary's yes that we do not pay attention to how she arrived at her answer. Take time now to look at all the verses in this reading again. See if you can identify steps of discernment that, even briefly, are noted here. List them, and extend them with your imagination. Then take some time to ponder the steps you take when confronted with a difficult, life-changing decision or promise. How do you discern your faithful response?

Your reflections—

DAY SIX

BEHOLD THE WAITING WORLD

Where in the world do you see youth at risk due to lack of guidance, protection, food, shelter, medical care, water, or hope? Be geographically specific with your responses. Where have you heard about young people, teens, youth around the world who live in dangerous, heartbreaking conditions? If you need to read some news sources to work with this question, do so. List at least three specific situations where young people are at risk somewhere in God's world and then consider what promises have been made and broken, and by whom, to put these young lives in hope-diminishing or death-dealing situations. What promises are being made or could be made by parents, friends, politicians, the church, community leaders, or others that could restore some hope to the future of these young people? How do you contribute on a personal level to any life-giving and hope-filled promises to young people in the world?

Your reflections—

DAY SEVEN

PRAYING AS PROMISE

My soul finds rest in God alone, my salvation comes from [God].

—PSALM 62:1, NIV

COMPLINE

Compline has been called by some a "bedtime" prayer. Its name derives from the Latin word *completorium*, which means "completion." It is intended to be a prayer that completes the day and that is followed by no conversation or last-minute activity other than departing in silence and going quietly to bed.

In Advent, the prayer practice of Compline offers important space to ponder the implications of God's promise made known in Jesus Christ. Imagine how good nightly rest must have felt to the young, expecting Mary. Busyness filled her days—visiting Elizabeth, traveling with Joseph, preparing to give birth—so to finally settle down to rest under roof or sky must have come as welcome respite from her upended daily life. Recall how at night Joseph received God's promise in a dream that the baby Mary carried was a child to be loved, cared for, and nurtured—not a child to be rejected. At night the holy family traveled and the holy star came to rest. At night the shepherds worked and wondered. At night the angels swooped and sang. The cover of night enfolded and revealed much of the Advent promise.

Little wonder that much of the church's Advent liturgical and worship life takes place at night. Something about scripture read in candlelight, music from the shadows, entering and departing a sanctuary under the night sky lends to the anticipation of Christmas Eve. And so, the prayer of Compline, Night Prayer, seems fitting to learn and practice during this season. A brief guide for Compline follows.

May night reveal and illumine for you God's promise of eternal love made known in Jesus the Christ.

A Guide to the Practice of Compline

People most often associate Compline, like all daily office liturgies, with a communal practice of prayer, but it is no less accessible for individuals who seek prayerful peace at the close of the day. Much of the language in the following Compline liturgy uses "we" and "us." Although you may wish to revise these words to "I" and "me" if praying in solitude, I instead encourage you to retain the plural to symbolize that we are never alone in prayer and always carry others with us.

This practice need not take more than fifteen minutes, although you may wish to extend the times of silence. Compline is intended to be quiet and restful. Select a night when you can follow this prayer near to your bedtime. Often, Compline is prayed at 7:00 PM or later. If you plan to pray as part of a small group gathering, try to have no errands or last-minute activities between prayer time and going to bed. It will be best to arrange for silence following the liturgy.

Select a space in which to pray that can be darkened, with just enough light to read. If possible, have candles available. If you will be praying with others, be sure they know the time and location. Also alert them before they come that silence will follow the prayers instead of conversation. You will need only one Bible, candles, a source of light by which everyone can read, and a copy of the liturgy for all participants.

Whether you plan to follow Compline alone or with a group, before the prayer time, select one passage from the readings suggested in the guide and mark the scripture so that you can find it easily.

When you are ready, gather in silence, light a candle[s], and settle into the quiet. Lead or follow the liturgy at a pace that feels right to you. If you are with a group, lead them in the responses.

If you are alone, read the responses as part of your prayers. Go slowly and leave ample silence for reflection.

A LITURGY FOR COMPLINE

Gathering and Silence

> O God, come to our assistance.
> O Lord, hasten to help us.
>
> The Lord Almighty grant us a restful night and peace at the last. Amen.

Psalm 4

> Answer me when I call, O God of my right!
> You gave me room when I was in distress.
> Be gracious to me, and hear my prayer.
>
> How long, you people, shall my honor suffer shame?
> How long will you love vain words, and seek after lies?
> But know that the LORD has set apart the faithful for himself;
> the LORD hears when I call to him.
>
> When you are disturbed, do not sin;
> ponder it on your beds, and be silent.
> Offer right sacrifices,
> and put your trust in the LORD.
>
> There are many who say, "O that we might see some good!
> Let the light of your face shine on us, O LORD!"
> You have put gladness in my heart
> more than when their grain and wine abound.
>
> I will both lie down and sleep in peace;
> for you alone, O LORD, make me lie down in safety.

Prayer of Confession, Examination of Conscience, Declaration of Pardon

> Holy God, receive and hear our confessions.

Silence for self examination and confession.

Lord, have mercy,
Christ, have mercy,
Lord, have mercy.
Amen.

Scripture Reading

Select one of the following: Jeremiah 14:9, 22; Matthew 11:28-30; Hebrews 13:20-21; 1 Peter 5:8-9*a*

Prayer of Thanksgiving

Sovereign God, you have been our help during the day, and you promise to be with us at night. Receive this prayer as a sign of our trust in you. Save us from all evil; keep us from all harm; and guide us in your way. We belong to you, Lord. Protect us by the power of your name, in Jesus Christ we pray. Amen.

Silence

The Lord's Prayer

Canticle of Simeon (Nunc Dimittis)[1]

Lord, now let your servant go in peace;
  your word has been fulfilled:
my own eyes have seen the salvation
  which you have prepared in the presence of all people,
a light to reveal you to the nations
  and the glory of your people Israel.

Blessing

May your unfailing love rest upon us, O Lord, even as we hope in you.

Depart in silence.

Notes

1. The United Methodist Hymnal, no. 225 (Nashville: The United Methodist Publishing House, 1989).

CHRISTMAS EVE

O Manger,
straw-strewn cradle in the night,
rough-hewn, muzzle-dampened space
where cattle feed, sparrows nest,
and cloth snags on splintered wood.
O simple feeding trough
for God's lowly beasts;
you are first bearer of Good News;
first container of Living Water, Bread of Life.
Come, clear out with a gust of father's breath
and mother's trembling touch;
make room to behold the promise of God.
Amen.

GUIDE FOR SMALL GROUPS

This Guide is designed for use during Advent for a series of four weekly group sessions. You can adapt the format for a one-hour, ninety-minute, or two-hour session. The pattern of prayer, reading, singing (optional), and sharing is the same in each session. After the first week, participants will know what to expect. A group size of eight to twelve is optimal, with one person designated as the facilitator/leader through the sessions.

BEFORE THE GROUP GATHERS

As long as the last of the four sessions takes place before Christmas Eve, the group can meet on any day of the week. The facilitator/leader will need to select a location and time for the sessions, obtain an Advent wreath or Christ candle to use, and assist participants in obtaining personal copies of *Behold!* in advance of the first session. Although no advance preparation is required of participants, they should be encouraged to use the daily readings in the book to enrich their own Advent experience as well as that of the group. Also, each participant will need to bring a Bible to each session, along with something to write in.

PREPARING FOR THE SESSIONS

Leader preparation is minimal: setting up the space with chairs and Advent wreath (or Christ candle), contacting group participants regarding schedule and needed materials, and reading over the week's materials so that content for the session is selected and familiar. Each session includes a suggested hymn; the leader can either lead this as a reading or arrange for someone to serve as a song leader (this comes early in each session). Group participants need only to arrive on time and in an attitude of prayer, each bringing a copy of *Behold!*, a Bible, and a journal or notebook.

Setting Up for the Sessions

The leader should plan to arrive at least ten minutes before the session begins in order to make sure that the room is comfortable and ready, including the Advent wreath or candle that will be used. If the participants do not know one another, name tags would be helpful. The leader should be prepared to welcome participants as they arrive.

Elements of Each Session

Instructions for the one-hour or ninety-minute format, as well as a note (*) regarding a two-hour format.

Gathering and welcome (3–5 minutes)
Leader welcomes all; before group begins, leader reminds participants that during the conversation times, sharing aloud is never a requirement and participants may always "pass." The leader also stresses the importance of holding the sharing in these group sessions as confidential.

Lighting the Advent wreath candles (1 minute)

Invocation for the week by leader (1 minute)
(Use invocation for current week from pages 25, 43, 63, and 83.)

Hymn of the week, sung or read in unison (3–5 minutes)
(Use hymn for current week from pages 27, 45, 65, and 85.)

Silence (1 minute)

Introduction of word for the week by leader (1–2 minutes)
Leader reads aloud the word for the week, followed by a brief time of silence, then reads the word a second time.

Group reflection on the word (15–20 minutes)
Leader invites participants to turn in their books to the opening questions for the word of the week (pages 22, 40, 60, and 80). Using one or more of these questions, the leader begins a time of group sharing. Participants are invited to listen to one another and to allow time for all who want to share.

Silence (1 minute)

*Scripture reading and reflection (30–45 minutes)
Leader, in advance of the session, selects one scripture reading from Day Two, Three, Four, or Five of the current week. First, participants are asked to turn to the pages where this reading and its reflection exercise are located and are given 10–15 minutes to read or reread the material silently, making notes as desired. Then, when individual time ends, the leader facilitates a group sharing time (30–45 minutes) about insights or questions arising from the scripture and reflection.

Prayers of the Participants (5 minutes)
Leader asks for prayer requests, urging participants to include prayers for the world and its people.

The Lord's Prayer in unison (2 minutes)

Benediction by Leader (1 minute)
(Use benediction for current week from pages 28, 46, 66, and 85.)

Depart in peace

---

*For a two-hour format, one or more additional scripture readings and reflections may be added at this time, using the same format.

RESOURCES

Bauman, Lynn C. *The Anglican Rosary.* Telephone, TX: Praxis, 2001.

Eslinger, Elise S., comp. and ed. *Upper Room Worshipbook: Music and Liturgies for Spiritual Formation.* comp. and ed.. Nashville, TN: Upper Room Books, 2006.

Dawson, Gerrit Scott; Adele Gonzalez; E. Glenn Hinson; Rueben P. Job; Marjorie J. Thompson; and Wendy M. Wright. *Companions in Christ: A Small-Group Experience in Spiritual Formation*, Participant's Book. Nashville, TN: Upper Room Books, 2001.

Doerr, Nan Lewis, and Virginia Stem Owens. *Praying with Beads: Daily Prayers for the Christian Year.* Grand Rapids, MI: William B. Eerdmans, 2007.

Funk, Mary Margaret. *Tools Matter for Practicing the Spiritual Life.* New York: Continuum International, 2004.

Job, Rueben P., and Norman Shawchuck. *A Guide to Prayer for All God's People.* Nashville: Upper Room Books, 1990.

___. *A Guide to Prayer for All Who Seek God.* Nashville, TN: Upper Room Books, 2003.

Job, Rueben P., ed. *Becoming a Praying Congregation: Churchwide Leadership Tools.* Nashville, TN: Abingdon, 2009.

___. *When You Pray: Daily Practices for Prayerful Living.* Nashville: Abingdon, 2009.

Killinger, John. *Beginning Prayer.* Rev. ed. Nashville, TN: Upper Room Books, 1993.

The Meeting God Bible: Growing in Intimacy with God through Scripture. New Revised Standard Version. Nashville, TN:

Upper Room Books, 1999, 2008. Published in partnership with HarperCollins Publishers.

Pathways Center for Spiritual Leadership. "A Guide to Daily Prayer." Nashville, TN: The Upper Room. (See pages 105–107.)

Skinner, Richard. *Invocations: Calling on the God in All.* Glasgow: Wild Goose Publications, 2005.

Thompson, Marjorie J. *Soul Feast: An Invitation to the Christian Spiritual Life.* Louisville, KY: Westminster John Knox Press, 1995.

Winston, Kimberly. *Bead One, Pray Too: A Guide to Making and Using Prayer Beads.* Harrisburg, PA: Morehouse Publishing, 2008.

Online resources for prayer beads
http://www.arosaryforall.com

http://www.cokesbury.com

http://www.episcopalbookstore.com

http://www.praxisofprayer.com

http://www.solitariesofdekoven.org

A Guide to Daily Prayer

Morning Prayer

"In the morning, O Lord, you hear my voice;
in the morning I lay my requests before you
and wait in expectation."

—Psalm 5:3

Gathering and Silence

Call to Praise and Prayer
God said: Let there be light; and there was light.
And God saw that the light was good.

Psalm 63:2-6

God, my God, you I crave;
my soul thirsts for you,
my body aches for you
like a dry and weary land.
Let me gaze on you in your temple:
a Vision of strength and glory
Your love is better than life,
my speech is full of praise.
I give you a lifetime of worship,
my hands raised in your name.
I feast at a rich table
my lips sing of your glory.

Prayer of Thanksgiving

We praise you with joy, loving God, for your grace is better than life itself. You have sustained us through the darkness: and you bless us with life in this new day. In the shadow of your wings we sing for joy and bless your holy name. Amen.

Scripture Reading

Silence

Prayers of the People

The Lord's Prayer (see Midday Prayer for text)

Blessing
> May the light of your mercy shine brightly on all who walk
> in your presence today, O Lord.

Midday Prayer

> "I will extol the LORD at all times;
>> God's praise will always be on my lips."
>> —Psalm 34:1

Gathering and Silence

Call to Praise and Prayer
> O LORD, my Savior, teach me your ways.
>> My hope is in you all day long.

Prayer of Thanksgiving
> God of mercy, we acknowledge this midday pause of refresh-
> ment as one of your many generous gifts. Look kindly upon
> our work this day; may it be made perfect in your time. May
> our purpose and prayers be pleasing to you. This we ask
> through Christ our Lord. Amen.

Scripture Reading

Silence

Prayers of the People

The Lord's Prayer (ecumenical text)
> Our Father in heaven,
>> hallowed be your name,

your kingdom come,
    your will be done,
    on earth as in heaven.
Give us today our daily bread.
Forgive us our sins as we forgive
    those who sin against us.
Save us from the time of trial,
    and deliver us from evil.
For the kingdom, the power, and the glory
    are yours, now and forever. Amen.

Blessing
Strong is the love embracing us, faithful the Lord from morning to night.

Evening Prayer

"My soul finds rest in God alone;
    my salvation comes from God."
                                —Psalm 62:1

Gathering and Silence

Call to Praise and Prayer
    From the rising of the sun to its setting,
        let the name of the Lord be praised.

Psalm 134
    Bless the Lord,
        all who serve in God's house,
        who stand watch
        throughout the night.
    Lift up your hands
        in the holy place
        and bless the Lord.

And may God,
    the maker of earth and sky,
    bless you from Zion.

Prayer of Thanksgiving

Sovereign God, You have been our help during the day and you promise to be with us at night. Receive this prayer as a sign of our trust in you. Save us from all evil, keep us from all harm, and guide us in your way. We belong to you, Lord. Protect us by the power of your name, in Jesus Christ we pray. Amen.

Scripture Reading

Silence

Prayers of the People

The Lord's Prayer (see Midday Prayer for text)

Blessing

May your unfailing love rest upon us, O LORD,
    even as we hope in you.

This Guide to Prayer was compiled from scripture and other resources by Rueben P. Job and then picked up by the Pathways Center for Spiritual Leadership while under the direction of Marjorie J. Thompson.

About the Author

Pamela C. Hawkins is a writer, artist, and United Methodist pastor. She has published two other books, *Simply Wait: Cultivating Stillness in the Season of Advent* and *The Awkward Season: Prayers for Lent*, as well as contributed to *Becoming a Praying Congregation*. From 2007 to mid-2011, Pamela served as managing editor of *Weavings: A Journal of the Christian Spiritual Life*, a publication of Upper Room Ministries. In June of 2011 she returned to local church ministry as an associate pastor of Belmont United Methodist Church in Nashville, Tennessee, where she and her husband, Ray, live.

CONTINUE YOUR COMMITMENT
TO DAILY SPIRITUAL PRACTICE

Let

The Upper Room
daily devotional guide

strengthen your faith in
God's love and infinite wisdom.

The Upper Room is unique among sources for daily
devotion; each reading is accompanied by a personal
commentary and a prayer by one of our readers. Every
day you'll be connected to a devout Christian community of nearly three million worshipers throughout the world.

Subscribe to *The Upper Room*
$12.00 for 1 year (6 issues)
Ask for Offer Code **AIDSBK**

Subscriptions sent outside the U.S. and its protectorates are
$20.00 per year and must be prepaid.

Order online at
www.upperroom.org
or call 800.972.0433